MW00975715

GITTIN' OFF ZERO.

THE STARTING POINT OF ONES GOALS, ASPIRATIONS AND DREAMS

gittinoffzero.com

GITTIN' OFF ZERO

Courtney R. Brown JR.

"Still I Rise" by Maya Angelou

"You may write me down in history
With your bitter, twisted lies,
You may trod me in the very dirt
But still, like dust, I'll rise.

Does my sassiness upset you?
Why are you beset with gloom?
'Cause I walk like I've got oil wells
Pumping in my living room.

Just like moons and like suns,
With the certainty of tides,
Just like hopes springing high,
Still I'll rise.

Did you want to see me broken?
Bowed head and lowered eyes?
Shoulders falling down like teardrops
Weakened by my soulful cries.

Does my haughtiness offend you?
Don't you take it awful hard
'Cause I laugh like I've got gold mines
Diggin' in my own back yard.

You may kill me with your hatefulness,
But still, like air, I'll rise.

Does my sexiness upset you?
Does it come as a surprise
That I dance like I've got diamonds
At the meeting of my thighs?

Out of the huts of history's shame
I rise
Up from a past that's rooted in pain
I rise
I'm a black ocean, leaping and wide,
Welling and swelling I bear in the tide.
Leaving behind nights of terror and fear
I rise
Into a daybreak that's wondrously clear
I rise
Bringing the gifts that my ancestors gave,
I am the dream and the hope of the slave.
I rise
I rise
I rise.

GITTIN' OFF ZERO

If this book was purchased with a "dull' or missing cover on it, please beware that neither the Author nor the publisher has received payment; you, the consumer, may have obtained an illegal copy of this book. Please contact the Publisher.

Gittin' Off Zero© 2014 Big Boss Filmworks

All rights reserved. Be advised that no part of this book may be reproduced, stored in or introduced into a retrieval system or transmitted in any form, electronic, mechanical, photocopying or otherwise without written permission from the publisher.

First Print- November 2014

ISBN- 978-0-9828506-1-9

Cover Concept: Courtney R. Brown Jr.
Graphic Design/Layout: Lewis Stevens
flyersplusgraphics.com 313.799.3325
Creative Consultant: Lewis F. Stevens
Editing: Raymond Tatum/Gittin' Off Zero Atlanta, Jacqueline Johnson

Big Boss Filmworks
P.O.Box 250464
Franklin, Michigan 48205

www.bigbossfilmworks.com
bigbossfilmworks@yahooo.com

DEDICATION

This book is dedicated to my parents, Theresa Brown and Courtney Brown Sr. It is said that to whom much is given, much is required; so very much is required of me because you both have given me so much. Having you as parents makes me believe I am the luckiest man alive. I thank God in heaven for both of you.

ACKNOWLEDGEMENTS

Natonya Bush Brown, my ex-wife; I thank you for continued pushing me to write this book and your constant reminders that people need to be motivated. You never let me forget the plight of the urban masses or the bright and talented people who just need some direction. Kimberly Brown, my sister, you are a great woman and even better sister. Aunt Sandra Poinsettia, you are the best. I love you and thank you for everything.

FAMILY

Prentiss, Pam, Melissa, Tammy, Cynthia, Jerry, Debra. To my niece, Alexis Farmer, you are the future of the family; Arthur Robinson, Art Jr. and family, Toni Robinson, Cornell, aka "La-La", Sincere April, Toni, Alice, The whole Robinson family, you are my blood. Aunt Carol, Aunt Colleen, Aunt Cheryl, Aunt Candace, Tammy, Jerry, Cynthia, Debra, Mike, Jamal, DeAnna, Michelle, Angela, Darren, Reggie, Ronald, Keith, Charles, Vincent, Craig, Darren, Aunt Charlotte's Boys. Cousin Cheryl, Karen, Buster, Denise, Hillard and Darius, Jay T, Pat, Natia, Stephanie and my whole Lakeland Florida family.

FRIENDS

Mark Talley, Nate Crimes, Eddie Jackson Jr., Jimmy Coleman, Craig Johnson, Chris Dyson and the Dyson family, Harry and Craig Todd, Cassandra Jackson aka Trisha. The Alpha Phi Alpha Frat '06, Quinton Webb, Eddie Fowlkes, Mike Kitchen, Walter Woods, Paul Thompson, Lenny Burnett, James and Gloria Johnson, Paul and Paula. Bill Hardy, you are a true friend and great mentor. Mr. Eugene Moore, Ivano Davis and Gear Unlimited, Charlie C., James R., Zack, aka "Rick", Mike Brock and the whole Detroit Fellowship; Pastor Wendell Anthony, Pastor Lee Andrew Jackson, Eva Whiteside, Lamont Bridges, Walter Haney, Young Choi, Sue Choi, Zac Binder, ATL, Terry, Frankie, Freddie and, of course, Sam Horne. Chuck Goldfarb, Al Profit and Scott Bernstein. Attorney Mc Manus- THANK YOU! FEDS Magazine, DeMayo and Una, Don Diva, Tony and Kevin Chiles (thanks for your words of wisdom). Danielle, Ms. Jackie Johnson, Harlem World's Ice. Special thanks to Russell Clayton Jr. and family for their energy and support Anita L. Flanagan. Special Thanks to Michelle Moore of Hood Books and the good people of Black and Nobel.

REST IN PARDISE

My Grandmother, Mae (I love you), Uncle Jay, Annie Mae McCleary, Darrell, aka Darrell T. Walker, Randy Murphy, Clifford aka "Freddie", Alice Robinson, Rosalind, Tony Robinson, Spencer Robinson, Aunt Connie, Aunt Charlotte, Refare, Poppa, Helen Garman; special memories of my great grandmother, Maggie Robinson aka "Momma", Margie Morris, my grandmother, Wipe Out, John Bailey, aka "John The Baptist", Daniel, Irving Goldfarb, Attorney Milton Henry, Attorney H. Ross Black and Elijah Jackson, Eddie Jackson's brother and cofounder of the empire (your mark has not been forgotten)Theresa and Theresa's Place.

BEHIND THE SCENES

Special thanks to Jackeline Johnson. Without your editing and coaching, this project might not have happened. Thank you and you are not forgotten. Lastly but not leastly; thank you for 35 years of mentorship and friendship. Thank you always.

Lewis Stevens, you have been, and are, my right-hand man on this project and all Big Boss Filmworks projects. Thank you for all you do.

To Annie Stevens, Lew's grandmother thanks for the use of your home and your support in general. The French Road crew, William and Brue Harmon; Karen

Stevens and Omar Lee, Lew's parents (your talks and positive energy kept us working).

I have had such a blessed life and had so many great relationships and family ties that I would be thanking folks throughout the entire book. If you are one of those people who have touched my life and have not been mentioned, please blame it on my head and not my heart. I thank and love you all. All thanks and praises to God ...

Courtney R. Brown Jr.

Raymond Tatum
Founder of Gittin' Off Zero, Inc.

ACKNOWLEDGMENTS

*First, I thank GOD .

*My Mother Mrs., Lena Jones Tatum for all her LOVE and commitment to all her children, thank Mother, RIP. *To my Father Ozzie King Tatum Sr. without him there would be no me, RIP. *My sisters and brothers *(Susie Tatum Byrd, RIP) and brother in-law Joe Byrd, *Curtis Tatum and sister in-law Laverne Daniel Tatum, *Ozzie King Tatum Jr. and sister in-law Mary Ann Tatum, *Mary E. Tatum and (Wilson Bernard, RIP), *Reginald Tatum and sister in-law Karen Williams Tatum. *My Children's, Daughter: *Tammy L. Tatum Brooks and son in-law Anthony R. Brooks, Son: *Raymond Tatum Jr. *My granddaughters, *Ariel D. Brooks, *Madison A. Brooks,*Kennedy S. Brooks*Niece and Nephews, *Tiffany Tatum Waters, *Decarlo J. Tatum, *

(Anthony Tatum RIP), *Christopher Bernard. *Reginald Tatum Jr. *Reynard k. Tatum, *Rashaad k Tatum. *My great Nephews, *Decarlo J. Tatum Jr. *Demario J. Tatum, *Jeremiah R. Tatum, *Jeffery cook, *Dejon Waters. Reynard K Tatum Jr. *My first and second Cousins, *(John L. Jones RIP), *Eutha L. Jones *Hankerson *Charlie Thomas *Edward Thomas, *Mathew Thomas, *Leon Thomas, *Mary A. Thomas *(Douglas m. Thomas RIP), *Glenn Rushin, *Ruth A. Rushin Elliott, *Jacquelyn Rushin, *Vanessa L. Rushin, *Sharr R. Elliott Hill , *H. Preston Elliott Jr. *To all the Blackwell family, a special thanks to *Mrs, Indianna Blackwell, *(Brenda Blackwell Sampson, RIP), *Bernice Blackwell Burdette, *Anne Blackwell, thank you guys for your support in the beginning.*Jessie cup Davis RIP, *Bruce Wideman RIP, *L. Ivan Welch RIP, *Alvin C. pope, *Patricia A. Avery *Ulysses Fat pig Crawford, Eric (New York Shorty) and Julia Hardeman *Percy Headquarters Jones, *Sean X. Gumby, *Frank Miller, *Larry Miller, *Jerome Lawrence, *Jerome Jackson, *Charles Willis, *North Woodall, *Poka Jones, (*Gene T. Keith R.I.P.), *Michael C. Jenkins, (*James Tate R.I.P) and Gwendolyn Demple Cade, *James Smith, *Rodney Bowles, *A special thanks to Ronda Hinton, *Jule Lassiter, *Alvin Stafford , *Jennifer Stone, *Louis & Janice Richmond, *John Richardson, *(Rodney Allen, University of Chicago),

*Douglas Dean, *The Summerhill Community in ATL, *The Recovery Community in the ATL, *GMHCN In Decatur, Ga, *Double Trouble in recovery, *The Georgia Peer Specialist Program and all its graduates, especially my class 2009 *All the members of the world famous Highland Club in the ATL., *The next level hat shop in the ATL, *Evolve Clothier of Ga, *Best tee's in the ATL, *All my Facebooks, Instagram and Twitter Friends, *Luther Judson Price High School Alumni especially the Class of 1968.

A special thanks to Courtney R. Brown Jr, of Big Boss Film Works and High Exposure Consulting.

I meet Courtney in 2006 at his apparel store on Memorial Drive in Decatur Ga. The store was call Head &Toe and that's where our business relationship begin, he allowed me to put some GITTIN' OFF ZERO apparel in the store on consignment and from that relationship and business agreement The seed of this book was planted and with profound gratitude to Courtney from me for choosing to call the title of this book GITTIN' OFF ZERO, Thanks again PLAYER

.*If I missed any of my supporters please charge it to the lack of space and not my heart, GOD BLESS.

TABLE OF CONTENTS

Introduction (A People in Crisis)..15

Chapter 1 – When We Were Kings ....…….......21

Chapter 2- The Curse of Integration..27

Chapter 3 - Family Is the Glue...36

Chapter 4 – Return to the Motherland ....………....42

Chapter 5 – Get You Mind Right..47

Chapter 6 – Black Boardrooms...59

Chapter 7 - A Call to Duty 66

Chapter 8 – Vote or Die Trying...71

Chapter 9 - Standards... 76

Chapter 10 – Conclusion 82

Gittin' Off Zero

Introduction

"A People in Crisis" Courtney R. Brown JR.

"Start where you are with what you've got and you will find you have all you need."

-Booker T. Washington

"Preparing in 1953 to attack the Moncada barracks to start the Cuban revolution with a handful of men, Fidel Castro and his followers read over and again the story of how the great Black Cuban general, Antonio Maceo, had championed Cuba's war of liberation against Spain. Castro later wrote of his fighters' studies in a letter: Homer's Iliad contains no events more heroic, and our Mambis (Cuban independence fighters in the war against Spain) seem more legendary than they, Achilles less invincible than Maceo. Why must we live in ignorance of our great feat....? If children were to grow up exposed to such examples and inspired by those great souls, who could ever subjugate them."

Randall Robinson – Unbroken Agony

GITTIN' OFF ZERO

I recently saw a special on the BBC British Broadcast Company about some Blacks in Cuba who discovered a song they were singing originated in Sierra Leone, West Africa. Meaning that those Black Cubans were descendants of the people from Sierra Leone; they interviewed one Black Cuban. Who was proud and happy to finally know from what country his family originated. It's important for all people to know their family's roots, if that person is to have a healthy sense of self-esteem. To quote Jay Z, "you are blind baby, blind to the fact of who you are maybe my blood lines crazy! We got kings and queens and Michael Jordan Rings…"

There are more African American men in jail than in college. The unemployment rate among African American men in most major cities is 70%. The African American infant mortality rates are at third world levels. How did we get here? Could these statistics apply to the descendants of the great West African king, Mansa Musa the controller of the world's gold and salt distribution of his day, or to the descendants of Detroit's Black Bottom, The Harlem Renaissance or Black Wall Street in Tulsa, Oklahoma?

Hi, I am Courtney R. Brown Jr., C.E.O of Big Boss Filmworks, Big Boss Books, Isaiah Properties, African Nights INC., High Exposure Consulting and a consultant for Bridgefort, INC., a family business. You may ask, Why so many companies? Well, in today's world a man or woman may need to have 3 or 4 hustles or AKA enterprises to be able to live the lifestyle they want. The advantage of this is that when one enterprise aka hustle slows, another will be busy. Seldom will all the enterprises be slow at the same time. In the stock market they call it diversification. We at Big Boss Books and Big Boss Filmworks have decided to do this project in conjunction with High Exposure Consulting and GITTIN' OFF ZERO Atlanta because of the current state of many African American youth in our major cities, Detroit, Michigan in particular. Why Detroit? Well, two reasons: Firstly, I'm from Detroit and secondly, the current state of senseless murders along with its nation's leading unemployment rate makes Detroit a perfect case study. I will use life lessons and skills sets that I have obtained over the course of my life.

Why am I qualified to speak on these subjects? What insights do I have in transforming the street hustler's mentality into a legitimate business model? Let me give you all some background on me. My father was a major part of one of the nation's largest drug rings in American history. For more details see: "Motown Mafia" by yours truly Courtney R Brown Jr. bigbossfilmworks.com.

I grew up in the plush suburbs after my family moved from the projects. My family then was able to live the life of luxury from profits of my father's involvement in the underworld. When I say I understand the streets, take my word for it. My father was eventually sent to Federal prison. So when I say I know the downside of the streets, take my word for it.

I've managed a 12 million dollar year store in New York City. I've worked on the nation's most prestigious shopping streets. I graduated from Western Michigan and attended five other colleges. I've owned and

operated businesses in Harlem, New York, Atlanta, Georgia and Detroit, Michigan. I introduced the Joe Boxer and Coogi apparel lines to Harlem, New York. I've done business in China, Europe and the Caribbean. I've traveled the world vacationing. When I say I understand start up business and how international trade changed the world for all of us, take my word for it.

Enough about me - let's talk about you. Are you or your brother, sister, father, mother, aunt, uncle or family suffering from the effects of the country's latest recession and if you are African American you know that for many it's like the Great Depression. Unemployment among Black men range between 30-70% depending on whose stats you use.

I'm going to use Detroit as an example but these conditions can be applied to Philly, LA, Atlanta or any other big city in America. To understand where we are, we must understand where we came from. A people without an understanding of its history are people with no future.

Let's Git Off Zero!

CHAPTER I

"WHEN WE WERE KINGS"

"The Fall Of The Black Man"

"In history, of course, the Negro had no place in this curriculum. He was pictured as a human being of the lower order, unable to subject passion to reason, and therefore useful only when made the hewer of wood and the drawer of water for others. No thought was given to the history of Africa except so far as it had been a field of exploitation for the Caucasian. You might study the history as it was offered in our system from the elementary school throughout the university,
and you would never hear Africa mentioned except in the negative. You would never thereby learn that Africans first domesticated the sheep, goat, and cow, developed the idea of trial by jury, produced the first stringed instruments, and gave the world its greatest boon in the discovery of iron. You would never know that prior to the Mohammedan invasion about 1000
A.D. these natives in the heart of Africa had developed powerful kingdoms which were later organized as the Songhai Empire on the order of that of the Romans and boasting of similar grandeur."

Dr. Carted G Woodson – The Mis-Education of the Negro

 For a moment let's go back in history-way back like 700 years ago. In the year 1325 over 697 years ago a Black African king named Mansa Musa controlled a West African empire in what is today's Ghana and Mali and most of Nigeria. This Black king's empire was a gold empire. Mansa Musa sold gold to the White Europeans, Arabs and Asians of the world. The Black Africans of this day set the price of gold by which most of the world's economies were supported. In fact, until 40 years ago, the American economy was on the gold standard. This means the dollars in your purse or wallet were backed up by the gold held in places like Fort Knox, Kentucky.

Yes, 90 years before Columbus landed in the Americas and 300 years before the first slaves from Africa reached the shores of Virginia, Black men in West Africa were masters of the gold and salt supplies of the world. Yes! Black people have been in love with gold for a very, very long time.

Mansa Musa's West African Empire fell due to internal family fighting and conflicts with other major African tribes. These events weakened all of West Africa to a point where Europeans and Arab Asians

23

Mansa Musa

came in and took control of the land, which were some of the largest empires the world has ever known.

I believe that one of African American's biggest problems is that we begin with our history with our forefathers as slaves. If all you know about your history is that at one time Blacks were slaves in the American South, then Lincoln freed the slaves, then Dr. Martin Luther King, marched and now Obama is President, If that is your timeline, there is no wonder why so many Blacks do not know where they're going, because they don't know where they're from. I believe that if more Blacks knew that it was Black men that built the great pyramids and Sphinx in Egypt, which by the way is in Africa, and knew that Black people gave the Greeks and Arabs their math and science; that great Black kings in West Africa once ruled the world's gold resources then Blacks would feel better about themselves and would do better for themselves. Black people know more and talk more about the British royal family's history than about the royal families of Africa that once reigned supreme. I know my roots run way beyond the members of my family that were once slaves; I know that my roots go back to greatness, so I strive for greatness.

Did you know the great people of England were once

slaves to the Romans, or that the Black Moors once controlled Spain and half of France? Still, the once enslaved English people went on to create the British Empire "which the sun never sets upon". The people in England are taught that yes once they were slaves but then went on to control the world. African Americans must know that yes, we were slaves but we as a people also once were great rulers of many parts of the world. If you do your homework, you will find the fingerprints of the Black man in the history of China, Europe, Asia and South America.

Ok, back to how we got here. Once Mansa Musa's empire fell, many of the great Black kings' empires, such as Songhai, fell. Africa was weakened to a point where the Portuguese, Spanish, English, French and Dutch came in and pitted one Black king against the other, allowing for the horrible Atlantic slave trade to begin - The Middle Passage: That dreadful boat ride where Africans were kidnapped and forced to endure on the way to North and South America. This is one of the great mass murders in human history!

We will not spend more time on the next 400 years of slavery in America, the Caribbean and South America or the physical and mental damages done to Black people. Just think of the millions of Black women raped, the millions of Black men killed, and millions of Black children made orphans. Try to conceive the damage done. The effects of slavery that still haunt African Americans is a topic which would take years to discuss. The point is this: trading in diamonds, gold and doing business has always been a part of Black peoples make up. The difference is that in Mansa Musa's day, Black men controlled the world's gold, diamond and salt trades. Today Black men in Africa don't control the commodities we love so much. Today Black men in America mainly consume, at retail prices, the same gold that their forefathers once owned.

You might say to yourself that the slave experience robbed Blacks of their entrepreneurial roots. That is partially true. History tells us that is not all the facts. We will examine three different examples of Black communities thriving in business and culture after slavery.

Let's GIT OFF ZERO!

CHAPTER 2

<u>THE CURSE OF INTERGRATION</u>

"The White Man's Ice is colder than the Black Man's Ice"

-From the hood

Sarah Breedlove (December 23, 1867 – May 25, 1919), known as **Madam C. J. Walker**, was an American entrepreneur and philanthropist, regarded as the first female self-made millionaire in America. She made her fortune by developing and marketing a successful line of beauty and hair products for black women under the company she founded, Madam C. J. Walker Manufacturing Company.

What a phrase Black Wall Street brings to mind - a picture of Black bankers and Black captains of industry. You might be thinking to yourself that one day we will have a Black Wall Street. The fact is we already had a Black Wall Street. World famous Booker T Washington saw this thriving community and labeled it Black Wall Street. Black Wall Street is what Tulsa, Oklahoma from 1830 -1921 was called. During this era, Blacks in Tulsa, Oklahoma had developed a business community that was booming; brothers and sisters were living large. Some Blacks profited from the booming oil business and others from service businesses such as doctors, lawyers, bankers, dry cleaners or insurance companies. There were a large number of Black banks in Tulsa. The Black dollar was said to circulate seven times among Black hands before it left the Black community. This means to say if you were a Black carpenter in Tulsa during these times your money would be circulating something like this: a Black carpenter does some home repairs for a Black lawyer; the Black lawyer pays the Black carpenter for the home repairs. That is the Black dollar moving one time between Blacks. The Black carpenter then takes his pay and deposits half of it in a Black owned bank. This is the Black dollar exchanging hands twice among Blacks.

GITTIN' OFF ZERO

The Black carpenter takes some of his remaining pay and

Black Wall Street, Tulsa , OK

takes his family to dinner at a Black owned restaurant. That is the Black dollar changing hands three times. The Black restaurant owner uses some of the money from the dinner plate; he sold to the carpenter, to pay his staff who are the Black waiters and Black bartenders. That is four times the same Black dollar has been circulated among Blacks in Tulsa. The Black Staff then uses some of their pay to go shopping at a Black owned clothing store. That is now 5 times that this currency has changed hands between Blacks. The Black clothing store owner then uses the profits of his sales to expand his store which leads to him hiring the same Black carpenter to do the remodeling. We are now at six times that the Black dollar in Tulsa has been exchanged within the black community.

The carpenter hires the same Black lawyer that started this cash cycle to do the carpenter's contract paperwork. This scenario has been used by every ethnic group to prosper in America. Of course when you play out this scenario the lawyer's son may marry the carpenter's daughter and the community's money is never far away.

Now let's think about Detroit or other large American cities, if a Black male or female is lucky enough to have a job, when they get paid, let's say from the local mall which is owned by a person likely from the Middle East or Asia, they cash their checks at a local check cashing store for a

George Washington Carver

small fee. Then they go shopping at footlocker and get some food at T.G.I. Friday's and buy some gas from a gas station, which is also owned by someone from the Middle East. Once that African American is paid, no money is likely to be spent with another Black business owner. Maybe the local barber or beauty Shop will see a small fraction of those wages.

This creates two big problems: Firstly, the money that is made in the hood never stays in the hood. So the hood becomes a desert for businesses outside of life's basic needs: gas, lights, utility, because, the owners of the majority of businesses in most cities with large Black population do not live in those cities. So no money circulates within those cities. For example, I own a gas station on a major street in Detroit. But I live 40 miles outside the city. The profits from my gas station will be spent 40 miles outside of the city. I will shop and entertain myself near where I live, which is far from the city. Let's stop here for a moment. I know some of you are reading and saying that I am talking about all the Arab or Korean businesses in the hood. You know they make all that money in the hood but don't spend any of their profits there.

Yes, it is true in Detroit and most other major cities with a large Black population. Most of the businesses in the Black community are owned and operated by people from the Middle East or Asia but we as African Americans should not be angry or hate these people or have any negative feelings for them; let's be adult on this issue. The vast majority of those of Asian or Arab descent are mostly hard working men and women who came to America to find a way to feed their families. They could not speak English well so they could not get a good paying job; they took the worst low paying jobs and saved their money, opened up businesses pooling their talents and energy. If you know the history of the Arab or Korean or Chinese people you will know they are merchants all over the world not just in your city. It is in their culture to be business people; it has been that way for thousands of years. Read Thomas Sowell's book 'Black Rednecks' for more information.

On a personal note, in my business ventures it has been members of the Arab and Korean community that have had my back, loaned me money, and shared their worldwide connections. They are business people if you act like a business person they will do business with you. African Americans must seek out business partnerships with those of different backgrounds. My question is why we don't own more businesses in our community? Let's look, for examples to when Blacks owned and operated businesses in their community. It's Harlem, NY and as the great Black author Langston Hughes wrote, Harlem was "En vogue". The village of Harlem is a small section of New York City which was dominated by Blacks in the 1920s. It was also the heart of Black culture: jazz, bebop, and blues music thrived. Billie Holiday, the Beyoncé of that time often performed at Black clubs in Harlem. Ask yourself, when was the last time Jay Z or Beyoncé performed in a Black owned venue?

But the great lesson of 1925 Harlem is not that Blacks owned, operated and performed in their own clubs, but that Whites and all other ethnicities came and supported those clubs. Even today in Harlem, in places like Lennox Lounge or Sylvia's you might find Whites and Asians from around the world spending money to view live Black entertainers and eat soul food, at top dollar. My point is that the world has always marveled at the talents of Blacks and if we are to GIT OFF ZERO we must start marketing and distributing our God given talents. Such as: Baby of Cash Money Records, Jay Z

Bob Johnson

of Roc-a-fella records, Puffy of Bad boy and maybe the best example is Bob Johnson, the first black billionaire who founded BET television which later sold for over a billion dollars.

Harlem N.Y. circa '20s

In Detroit, in the 1940s, 50's, 60's there were two Black 5 star hotels: The Carson Plaza and The Gotham Hotel - they were as nice as any Marriott or Hilton. The Black elite of that day stayed and supported these hotels. Unless you are over 55 years of age, you have never seen or have been inside a Black five star hotel. Of course the era of the Black owned 5 star hotels was the area of segregation. When Blacks think of segregation and they immediately think of the Ku Klux Klan and separate drinking fountains for Blacks and Whites. It is true that from the end of slavery, in 1865 until 1965 the wall that kept Blacks and Whites separated allowed for the persecution of Blacks at many levels. The flip side of the segregation story is that it forced Blacks to mainly shop at Black owned businesses and also provided entertainment for themselves; allowing for many Black businesses to thrive. Remember, African Americans once had their own pro baseball, basketball, and football leagues.

As of today there is one Black owned professional sports team, Michael Jordan, of the Charlotte Hornets. Once the Blacks could get a room at the Marriott and Black ball players could play for the LA Lakers, Black ownership of sports teams and hotels disappeared. African Americans have become a people who take pride in making other cultures rich, while their communities fall apart. So many Blacks especially the youth take such pride in the communities they live aka 'hood'. In fact, at times these youths will kill in defense of their hood against any form of disrespect. Yet those very same youth care not about broken glass, graffiti, prostitute filled streets that dominate their hood. They care about a stranger selling a 10 dollar bag of weed on their block, but care not about a stranger selling all inferior food on their block. It seems that once Blacks could live next to Whites the care for the Black neighborhood seized to exist.

GITTIN' OFF ZERO

What moved to White dominated neighborhoods was the Black brain power and business skills needed to maintain safe clean neighborhoods. During segregation, Black doctors, lawyers, teachers, pimps, numbers men, and gangsters lived side by side, along with bus drivers, cops, and working people. This led to many stable financially prosperous Black neighborhoods. Whether this was the south side of Chicago, Black Bottom, Detroit, Harlem, New York and Black Wall Street Tulsa Oklahoma, a Black child grew up to see all phases of the Black experience, the good and bad. Today sadly, a little Black boy growing up in the center of the city sees too many Black men addicted to drugs, Black women as prostitutes and businesses owned by people who do not look like them. African Americans must follow the example of other successful minorities. Let's GIT OFF ZERO!

CHAPTER 3

<u>FAMILY IS THE GLUE THAT HOLDS ALL CUTURES TOGETHER</u>

"What Happened to Big Momma's House?"

Ask yourself, what has allowed Jewish Americans and Chinese Americans and yes even Jamaican American to thrive in America, even though they have language and cultural challenges that most Black families never faced. Well the key word is family. The common factor they have is an understanding that cash and education go hand in hand. If you have more shoes than books in your home, think about what message you're giving to your children.

GITTIN' OFF ZERO

Think about this: The grandchildren of slaves became the Tuskegee Airmen; the Black fighter Pilots that helped America win the Second World's War. The U.S. government recruited these Black pilots from colleges all over the country. If in two generations out of slavery Black Americans could produce some of the best pilots on the planet, how can it be in 2014, over 147 years after slavery, the Black high school dropout rate in many cities in America is over 50 percent? When the family unit falls apart the neighborhood or community will fall apart. There once was a time when Blacks like all other minorities or immigrants believed their life's work was to build a better life for the future generations. With planning and sacrifice, we once knew that although daddy is a garbage man and momma is a maid their kids could become doctors, lawyers or business people. Although there's a segment of the Black community that has continued the tradition of each generation doing better than the last, the majority of Black families in big cities are going backwards financially. As we stated earlier, when the Black doctor and lawyers moved out of the old Black neighborhoods after integration they took with them the family road map for success in America. Sixty years ago a struggling

Black family had hope because they had lots of examples of successful Blacks that came from struggling family backgrounds. There was a time when Black doctors, lawyers, teachers, gangsters and working men all lived in the same neighborhood. So as a youth growing up in that neighborhood, you saw all types of role models. I speak of the days in the Black community when each family felt a responsibility to each child in the neighborhood. Maybe you have heard some elders speaking of a time when if a child misbehaves on the block any neighbor might spank him or her and then take the child to their parents who would administer another spanking. Let's talk about today when a child curses in public or wears his pants hanging off of his ass, no one says anything. It is true what the African proverb says, "it takes a village to raise a child".

In Africa over the past 100 years, there has been what is called a 'brain drain'. That is to say, that the best and brightest

Africans have left Africa because of the lack of opportunities and corruption. If you live in London, Paris, New York, City or Chicago you may have come in contact with some of these smart, highly motivated Africans that have left Africa and moved to Europe or America and have done very well for themselves. That is good for them, but bad for Africa: Because what was left in Africa was a lot of young and old people with limited work skills. In so many cases the same problems that harms Africa harms inner city American Blacks.

In America, after the civil rights movement of the 50's 60's, there was a brain drain in large Black cities. The best and brightest left the cities for the suburbs. Leaving the inner cities void of role models and neighborhood leadership. Maybe there is the small business owner, or a teacher or two remaining in the hood, but mostly there are only single mothers raising families. Of course, we know that too many Black men are in jail or affected with other issues to help these single moms out -

GITTIN' OFF ZERO

We will address that problem later. Show me a culture with healthy families and I will show you a successful culture.

African Americans are in danger of losing the big mama or big papa figure; that being, the grandparent that was the family historian, the family judge and family source of stability. If grandmother is 45, momma is 30, and the granddaughter 15 and pregnant, it is difficult for that family unit to prosper. Notice there was no man in that scenario. The Black male / female relationship must become a healthy relationship or all the government handouts will not save the day. We can do it, one relationship at a time - lets GIT OFF ZERO!

"An average of one in two children in the U.S. grows up without a father; in the inner city, that increases to four in five. This has created a **mission field** right here in our cities, neighborhoods and even in our churches. Fatherless boys may feel that they have to toughen up, but deep down they may feel hurt, angry, intensely unhappy, ashamed and alone. These are the boys who desperately need male role models, mentors in their lives.

Fatherless America! How sad for a nation that once not only took pride in knowing the Heavenly Father, but also took pride in the strength of their families and their earthly fathers."

William Raspberry from the Washington Post once wrote: *"If I could offer a single prescription for survival of America it would be to restore the family. And if you asked me how to do it, my answer...doubtlessly over-simplified...would be: save the boys."*

Dr. Denis Kimbro – Daily Meditations

CHAPTER 4

Return to the Mother Land

"Go Where The Gold is"

Maybe you have heard the phrase 'globalization'. 'Globalization' is basically the exchange of goods and ideas on a global scale; the world has gotten very small. You ask yourself: How does that affect me back in the hood? Well, the reason why you can't get that customer service job or that job at the plant is because those jobs have been sent or outsourced to places like China and India. The news gets worse as the rest of Asia moves from farm to city and as Africa becomes more stable; there are billions of people willing to work and work hard for two or three dollars an hour. Do not believe the hype the jobs America has lost are not coming back!

China and India have been economic powers for most of human history; America is only 235 years old. So don't be surprised that other parts of the world are getting their share of the money pie. The biggest problem is that there are people in China, India and much of Asia that are educating their children in first-rate ways, while children here are trying to learn in unsafe overcrowded schools. Simply put, for all you young and not so young people, you are not competing for jobs with your friends or peers in your city or state; you're competing against the whole world. So as the kids say: "you better upgrade your game".

There's a silver lining to the rise of Asia, Africa, Brazil and Russia. That silver lining is that there are billions of people worldwide who never have had money to spend. They are now working and able to buy clothes, cars and computers. To take

Bob Johnson Liberia Sirleaf

advantage of this you must have clothes, cars and computers to sell to them. If you watch CNN, or any other worthwhile news network, you will hear them speak of BRIC nations.

BRIC nations stand for Brazil Russia India and China. These are the four fastest-growing economies on earth. These are the nation's that you must consider ways to do business with. The world has always loved Black culture: Our music, dress and

Liberian subway system

slang. African Americans must begin to cash in on our culture. Black Americans know the trends in music and fashion

before Wall Street or the fashion magazines. They must be willing to think outside the box. Yes it is great to open up a clothing store in the hood, I know, because I had many stores in the hood and local malls. But if wealth is what you want, you might want to save some money, get a passport, hop on a plane, and open up a business in Rio de Janeiro, Brazil. There are 40 million Blacks in America but there are over 80 million Blacks in Brazil. Once you get over your fear of change you can start making a lot of CHANGE. Africa, your motherland, also offers great opportunities – see ("Blacks without Borders") Documentary for more information. For Black Americans, I know that when you think of Africa, you think of little, naked, hungry, Black kids or civil

Bob Johnson's African Luxury Resort

wars. It is true that in many parts of Africa poverty still exists and many African Nations suffer from corrupt governments and international greed that leads to civil wars and social chaos. But there's another Africa. I've been to Ghana, Senegal, Nigeria, the Ivory Coast and Mauretania. I have traveled all over the world but the nicest beaches I've ever seen were in West Africa. There are night clubs, casinos, fashion, and beautiful people making lots of money in many parts of Africa. One of my company's, African Nights INC's main focus is doing business in Africa. We buy Shea butter and colorful fabrics imported from Africa and that's cool. What about Africa's massive gold silver, platinum, coffee, chocolate and rubber inventories?

Africa's fast growing middle class loves African American culture, fashion and music. African Americans love Africa's gold, silver, platinum and coffee yet there is very little trade

45

between these blood cousins. If you are an African American, you have relatives in Africa. I'm not saying you have to move to Africa to do business there; although for many Black Americans Africa has many more opportunities than in America. See - the documentary 'Africa Dollars or Danger'. Marcus Garvey set out a plan for Africans and Black Americans to trade but European and international business men who made billions raping Africa of its wealth, conspired to ruin Garvey and stop his plan. What Garvey knew was that he who controls Africa controls the resources and therefore controls much of the world's wealth. Don't sleep - Africa, Brazil and China offer life changing opportunities. It takes 18 hours to drive from New York to Atlanta; it takes 8 hours to fly from New York City to West Africa. With the price of gas today, the trip is very close in price. Once you embrace Africa, Brazil or China you will see the massive buying power of your U.S. dollars. In summary, the world has changed and become very small: read, travel, learn and get money; don't stay stuck on stupid. Jews travel to Israel, Irish travel to Ireland, Germans travel to Germany. So why would African Americans NOT travel to Africa? Do it and it will change your life and maybe your pockets. Let's GIT OFF ZERO!

CHAPTER 5

<u>GET YOUR MIND RIGHT</u>
"A Man Is As He Thinks."

" The lack of confidence of the Negro in himself and in his possibilities is what has kept him down. His mis-education has been a perfect success in this respect. Yet it is not necessary for the Negro to have more confidence in his own workers than in others. If the Negro would be as fair to his own as he has been to others, this would be all that is necessary to give him a new lease on life and start the trend upward. Here we find that the Negro has failed to recover from his slavish habit of berating his own and worshipping others as perfect beings. No progress has been made in this respect because the more "education" the Negro gets the worse off he is. He has just had so much longer to learn to decry and despise himself. The race looking to this educated class for a solution of its problems does not find any remedy; and, on the contrary, sees itself further and further away from those things to which it has aspired. By forgetting the schoolroom for the time being and relying upon

an awakening of the masses through adult education we can do much to give the Negro a new point of view with respect to economic enterprise and group cooperation. The average Negro has

not been sufficiently mis-educated to become hopeless. Our minds must become sufficiently developed to use segregation to kill segregation, and thus bring to pass that ancient and yet modern prophecy, "The wrath of man shall praise thee." If the

Negro in the ghetto must eternally be fed by the hand that pushes him into the ghetto; he will never become strong enough to get out of the ghetto. This assumption of Negro leadership in the ghetto, then, must not be confined to matters of religion, education, and social uplift; it must deal with such fundamental forces in life as make these things possible. If the Negro area, however, is to continue as a district supported wholly from without, the inept dwellers therein will merit and

will receive only the contempt of those who may occasionally catch glimpses of them in their

plight."

Dr. Carted G Woodson – The Mis-Education of the Negro

GITTIN' OFF ZERO

Life has taught me this simple lesson: Every day the world rewards people with knowledge and everyday it punishes people without knowledge. Simply put, the more a person knows about many things the easier life is; the less a person knows about different things the harder life is. One of my favorite rappers, the late great Christopher Wallace aka Biggie Smalls, had a line in one of his songs: 'Money, hoes and clothes, all a nigga knows". Although it is a very catchy line some youth in the Black community take that line's attitude to heart. You are a fool if you think an uneducated people can be a wealthy people. The motto of my consulting company, High Exposure Consulting, is "Knowledge is Power." Since no one seems to want to talk about it, I will. All over America there is a troubling trend that being cool is to be stupid. America's inner city youths drop out of high school, while smiling and laughing on their way to jail and the graveyard.

In America's rural areas working class people vote for tax cuts for billionaires and really believe somehow it will help their families. This is not a race issue. It is a survival issue - In today's world, math and science and a firm understanding of economics is fundamental to being able to provide for oneself and family. America's colleges and universities are still the envy of the world. However, our K - 12 schools are becoming the joke of the world.

If more Americans were better educated in the right areas,

50

many of our nation's issues would not exist. For example, the housing crisis; if more people had a simple understanding of supply and demand there would not have been a housing crisis. Detroit for example! From 2000 to 2007 home prices were rising in Detroit yet during the same period, Detroit's population was dropping quickly. Anyone who knows anything about business knows that price is determined by the balance of supply and demand. Example, many people want a Bentley car but there are only a few Bentleys made every year. Therefore, there's a high demand for Bentleys but a low supply, therefore the price is high. On the other hand, not many people want a 10 year old Ford Escort but there are many of them available so the price is low.

If the average Detroiter or its leadership understood the laws of supply and demand, they would have known that with a falling population the prices of the homes had to go down sooner or later. Of course it was sooner and now Detroit has an abundance of empty foreclosed homes, which destroy the city's tax base and realty market. It's that simple. If the average Detroit homeowner had read any business books or asked anyone what makes the price of things go up and down, they would never have taken on a $100,000 mortgage on a home whose true value was $35,000. They did not know and the world punished them for not knowing. It's hard to win at a game when you don't understand the rules.

Becoming financially independent is based on understanding the capitalist game. I believe Black Americans, and Americans in general, need a 180 degree turn in our view towards reading and education. We live in the era of reality TV and music videos. Society has too many toys to allow person to entertain themselves all day long and not learn anything of value. When you are engrossed in your favorite reality show or watching YouTube videos someone else is reading a book on money management, math, or science. Entertainment has its place in life but it should be dessert, not your main course! As the kids in the streets say, 'while you sleeping' on getting some education the rest of the world is on its grind, getting smarter and wiser. Who do you think wins the game of life? Get your mind right and GIT OFF ZERO.

"Several other reasons may be given for the failure of a larger number of Negro actors to reach a higher level. In the first place, they have been recognized by the white man only in parely plantation comedy and minstrelsy, and because of the large number entering the field it has failed to offer a bright future for many of such aspirants. Repeatedly told by the white man that he could not function as an actor in a different sphere, the American Negro has all but ceased to attempt anything else. The successful career of Ira Aldridge in Shakespeare was forgotten until recently recalled by the dramatic success of Paul Robeson in Othello. The large majority of Negroes have settled down, then, to contentment as ordinary clowns and comedians. They have not had the courage or they have not learned how to break over the unnatural barriers and occupy

higher ground. The Negro author is no exception to the
traditional rule. He writes, but the white man is supposed
to know more about everything than the Negro. So who
wants a book written by a
Negro about one? As a rule, not even a Negro himself, for
if he is really "educated," he must
show that he has the appreciation for the best in
literature. The Negro author, then, can neither
find a publisher nor a reader; and his story remains
untold. The Negro editors and reporters were
once treated the same way, but thanks to the uneducated
printers who founded most of our
newspapers which have succeeded, these men of vision
have made it possible for the "educated"
Negroes to make a living in this sphere in proportion as
they recover from their education and learn to deal with
the Negro as he is and where he is.

     Herein are recorded not opinions but the
reflections of one who for forty years has participated in
the education of the Black, brown, yellow and white races
in both hemispheres and in tropical and temperate
regions. Such experience, too, has been with students in
all grades from the kindergarten to the university. The
author, moreover, has traveled around the world to
observe
not only modern school systems in various countries but
to study the special systems set up by
private agencies and governments to educate the natives
in their colonies and dependencies.
Some of these observations, too, have been checked
against more recent studies on a later tour.

Discussing herein the mistakes made in the education of the Negro, the writer frankly admits that he has committed some of these errors himself. In several chapters, moreover, he specifically points out wherein he himself has strayed from the path of wisdom. This book, then, is not intended as a broadside against any particular person or class, but it is given as a corrective for methods which have not produced satisfactory results. The author does not support the once popular views that in matters of education Negroes are rightfully subjected to the will of others on the presumption that these poor people are not large taxpayers and must be content with charitable contributions to their uplift. The author takes the position that the consumer pays the tax, and as such every individual of the social order should be given unlimited opportunity to make the most of himself. Such opportunity, too, should not be determined from without by forces set to direct the prescribed element in a way to redound solely to the good of others but should be determined by the make-up of the Negro himself and by what his environment requires of him.

This new program of uplift, the author contends, should not be decided upon by the trial and error method in the application of devices used in dealing with others in a different situation and at another epoch. Only by careful study of the Negro himself and the life which he is forced to lead can we arrive at the proper procedure in this crisis. The mere imparting of information is not education. Above all things, the effort must result in making a man think and do for himself just

as the Jews have done in spite of universal persecution.
In thus estimating the results obtained from the so-called
education of the Negro the author does
not go to the census figures to show the progress of the
race. It may be of no importance to the
race to be able to boast today of many times as many
"educated" members as it had in 1865. If
they are of the wrong kind the increase in numbers will be
a disadvantage rather than an
advantage. The only question which concerns us here is
whether these "educated" persons are
actually equipped to face the ordeal before them or
unconsciously contribute to their own
undoing by perpetuating the regime of the oppressor

Herein, however, lies no argument for the oft-heard
contention that education for the white man
should mean one thing and for the Negro a different thing.
The element of race does not enter
here. It is merely a matter of exercising common sense in
approaching people through their
environment in order to deal with conditions as they are
rather than as you would like to see
them or imagine that they are. There may be a difference
in method of attack, but the principle
remains the same.
"Highly educated" Negroes denounce persons who
advocate for the Negro a sort of education
different in some respects from that now given the white
man. Negroes who have been so long
inconvenienced and denied opportunities for development
are naturally afraid of anything that

GITTIN' OFF ZERO

sounds like discrimination. They are anxious to have
everything the white man has even if it is
harmful. The possibility of originality in the Negro,
therefore, is discounted one hundred per cent
to maintain a nominal equality. If the whites decide to take
up Mormonism the Negroes must
follow their lead. If the whites neglect such a study, then
the Negroes must do likewise.
The author, however, does not have such an attitude. He
considers the educational system as it
has developed both in Europe and America an antiquated
process which does not hit the mark
even in the case of the needs of the white man himself. If
the white man wants to hold on to it, let
him do so; but the Negro, so far as he is able, should
develop and carry out a program of his own.
The so-called modern education, with all its defects,
however, does others so much more good
than it does the Negro, because it has been worked out in
conformity to the needs of those who
have enslaved and oppressed weaker peoples. For
example, the philosophy and ethics resulting
from our educational system have justified slavery,
peonage, segregation, and lynching. The
oppressor has the right to exploit, to handicap, and to kill
the oppressed. Negroes daily educated
in the tenets of such a religion of the strong have
accepted the status of the weak as divinely
ordained, and during the last three generations of their
nominal freedom they have done
practically nothing to change it. Their pouting and
resolutions indulged in by a few of the race
have been of little avail.

GITTIN' OFF ZERO

No systematic effort toward change has been possible, for, taught the same economics, history, philosophy, literature and religion which have established the present code of morals, the Negro's mind has been brought under the control of his oppressor. The problem of holding the Negro down, therefore, is easily solved. When you control a man's thinking you do not have to worry about his actions. You do not have to tell him not to stand here or go yonder. He will find his "proper place" and will stay in it. You do not need to send him to the back door. He will go without being told. In fact, if there is no back door, he will cut one for his special benefit. His education makes it necessary."

Dr. Carted G Woodson – The Mis-Education of the Negro

Recommended Reading

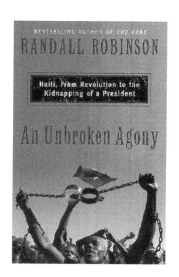

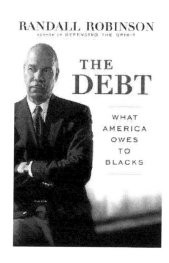

CHAPTER 6

BLACK BOARDROOMS

"Need a job? Start a business!"

GITTIN' OFF ZERO

"In the schools of business administration Negroes are trained exclusively in the psychology and economics of Wall Street and are, therefore, made to despise the opportunities to run ice wagons, push banana carts, and sell peanuts among their own people. Foreigners, who have not studied economics but have studied Negroes, take up this business and grow rich. "

-Carter G. Woodson
The MIs-education of the Negro

Necessity is the mother of invention. This well-known phrase implies that when one is in need of something, that need is the spark plug of new ideas and ways of doing things. What has made America a great nation is its entrepreneurial spirit, the willingness of men and women to bet on and invest in their own dreams and start a business. You're probably thinking, Mr. Brown is crazy when he says, "If you need a job then start a business." No, I need a 'for sure check' every two weeks. The problem with that logic is there's no such thing as a 'for sure check'. Secondly, the days of companies keeping employees around for 20 years are long gone.

 An 18 year old today will likely have over 10 jobs in his or her lifetime. Let's exam the word job; I say JOB stands for JUST OVER BROKE. There's a difference between a job and a career. When I think of a career, I think of nurses, doctors, corporate lawyers, plumbers, entrepreneurs or engineers. Most people who have those careers are paid well and enjoy their craft, although they may have a boss, they are rewarded for their expertise. If you work for someone doing something you don't like and think you are underpaid then you have a JOB, JUST OVER BROKE.

But as stated before knowledge is power. So if you want to one day own a restaurant it's a good idea to get a job at your local McDonalds or mom and pop diner. There you will learn the ins and outs of running a restaurant. You will be getting paid to learn how to run your own restaurant. I've owned and

operated a chain of clothing stores with many different concepts. I've had success in the clothing business. But what you must know is that almost every successful marketing and inventory control system, I used in my business, I learned from working for others. I've sold lots of sneakers on my own, but my first job was at the local mall in a place called Sneakers and Cleats. The owner of Sneakers and Cleats had started with one store, built his business into 5 stores, and then sold his business to a national chain. That lesson of starting a business, growing the business, and selling it to the big boys was one of the first and most important business lessons I learned. I have made a lot of money selling Coogi sweaters and Joe Boxer shorts, but before I sold them for myself, I managed a high end boutique owned by two Israeli businessmen. Those two Israeli businessmen taught me about the Coogi and Joe Boxer line of clothing. Their insights allowed me years later to sell the same lines they introduced me, to, in my own stores in the Black community and be successful. They were of Jewish origin.

My point is that you must be willing to work and learn from all types of people, if you want to advance in this world. If

62

you want to GIT OFF ZERO find something that interests you, then find someone who makes money from doing that. Observe them; maybe even work for them for free- just to get the knowledge. Remember, knowledge is power. One of my pass

On Set Motown Mafia

bosses told me a great truth about the business field. He said "Courtney, there is always room for one more: one more restaurant, one more clothing store or one more grocery store."

Don't let people kill your dreams when they tell you your business plan won't work because they're already too many businesses of a similar concept. McDonalds and Burger King were already large companies when Wendy's came along. It did not stop Wendy's from profiting because the fast food market is massive and there is always room for one more.

Even today new chains like Five Guys Burgers are opening new burger themes and making money. Remember, they print money every day all over the world. You can think of a way to get some of it. It will not be easy; it will take sacrifice, discipline, and many sleepless nights. But many of the good things in life require hard work discipline, sacrifice, and sleepless nights. The question is how bad do you want to GIT OFF ZERO?

Many of you may say;" I can't do that: what I need is a

job with benefits." I'm not suggesting everyone quit their job and start a business, but what I am saying is if you don't have a job or are in a profession like manufacturing; self-employment is something you should think about. We at High Exposure Life Coaching are here to help you make a plan. But do some homework on your own. Ask others who have GOT OFF ZERO how they did it.

Stop taking advice about business and money from people with NO money and NO business! I believe one of the greatest tragedies in the world is a person with no dreams. If the inner-city youth had more dreams, they would not do so many things that damage their lives and the people around them. Young, old and those in the middle should write down five things they want to do in life. Many of those things are going to require money. So let's GIT OFF ZERO and start chasing your dreams. As your president said, 'We are the help we are waiting for' – President Barack Obama

GITTIN' OFF ZERO

"It is very clear, therefore, that we do not have in the life of the Negro today a large number of persons who have been benefited by either of the systems about which we have quarreled so long. The numbers of Negro mechanics and artisans have comparatively declined during the last two generations. The Negroes do not proportionately represent as many skilled laborers as they did before the Civil War. If the practical education which the Negroes received helped to improve the situation so that it is today no worse than what it is, certainly it did not solve the problem as was expected of it.

-Carter G. Woodson
The Mis-education of the Negro

Chapter 7

A CALL TO DUTY

"Am I My Brother's Keeper?"

GITTIN' OFF ZERO

During the turn of the 20th century, German Jews had already made themselves strong economically and well accepted socially, in the USA. They were highly educated and sophisticated when Jews from Eastern Europe started to arrive in large numbers. These Jews were poorly educated and did not speak English well. In some ways they were an embarrassment to the prosperous German Jews. Well what did the Germans Jews do? Did they distance themselves from the unsophisticated Eastern European Jews out of shame? No, they reached back and used their wealth and knowledge of how America worked and quickly brought the Eastern European Jews up to speed and helped increase the wealth of all Jewish people.

GITTIN' OFF ZERO

LGG "Warm The Homeless"

This is but one example of what a united race or group of people can achieve, when those who have succeeded, reach back to those of their kind who are less fortunate. Successful African Americans, and America as a whole, have a question. The question is: What do we do with the urban masses and those stuck in a pattern of self-destructive living? Firstly, the African American upper class, who contrary to popular opinion make over a million dollars per year but are not sports figures or entertainers. They are doctors, lawyers and business people. Most of them are 2nd or 3rd generation success stories; the dysfunction and crime of the hood is far removed.

GITTIN' OFF ZERO

Yet, I believe they are the last best hope of African Americans trapped in failing schools and single mother homes. Successful African Americans should use their knowledge of organization and corporate structure to reengage the Black masses. There must be mentorship programs started on a massive nationwide scale. If we want young, Black boys to really know they have other option in life besides crime, rap music or sports, they have to see and hear from the many successful Black lawyers, doctors and business people first

hand. Black girls have to see and hear from the many successful Black women who have careers and families that know that life offers more than raising a family by themselves and exposing their children and themselves to dysfunction and a bleak future.

Although I have my issues with the NAACP and Urban League, they do have the infrastructure to serve as a bridge between the Black elite and the Black masses. Lastly, if the Black elite invested in the urban centers, they would reap massive profits along with being tangible role models. If you think there's no money in the hood, ask footlocker or McDonalds or your local liquor store owner. America as a whole, must address the growing gap between most of America and the top 1%. Never in America's history has so few controlled so much of the wealth. This is not a Black issue; it is an American issue. Black America must remember, you cannot be considered a great people if masses of your people are uneducated and poor. All of America must remember America cannot remain a great nation if the numbers of middle-class go down and the number of the poor increase.

African Americans and Americans as a whole are leaving many great young minds behind in the projects and trailer parks of America. Those are the minds America will need to compete in this competitive world. There's nothing wrong with helping someone GIT OFF ZERO.

CHAPTER 8

<u>VOTE OR DIE TRYING</u>

"Knowledge is Power"

"A few years ago a rather youthful looking high school principal in one of the large cities was unceremoniously dismissed because he said jocosely to the president of the board of education, in reply to his remark about his youthful bearing, "I am old enough to vote." "Horrors!" said the infuriated official. "Put him out. We brought him here to teach these Negroes how to work, and here he is thinking about voting," A few prominent Negroes of the place muttered a little, but they did nothing effective to correct this injustice. "

Carter G. Woodson – The Mis Education Of The Negro

Alabama voting line 1960's

Mississippi civil rights workers murdered 1964

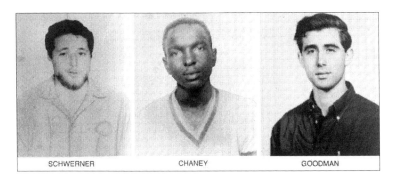

SCHWERNER   CHANEY   GOODMAN

March 29, 1961, in Jackson,

Mississippi. (AP Photo/Jackson Clarion-Ledger)

If you don't care about who your leaders are, you don't care about the direction of your city, state or nation. It never ceases to amaze me when people complain about the actions of politicians, yet do not vote or are not active in the election process. African Americans often suffer from the policies of people they had a chance to vote against, yet did not vote at all. In these challenging times, all wise people are interested in things like tax rates, Social Security and Medicare. These issues will affect all of America, but they will affect

African Americans the most. Those who know what the hood is like on the 1st of the month know how dependent many are on Social Security and Medicare. If there are even small cuts in those programs the pain in the hood will be great.

That said, with the stakes so high you would think people in the hood would have much more interest in the people who get elected and make those decisions. If the only time the masses of Black Americans are going to vote is when a Black man is running for president, the future is bleak. To GIT OFF ZERO you cannot have people in political office that want to keep you on zero. Surely, the rich make sure that politicians are not elected that would support policies that would threaten their wealth. I am trying to school you to the game of politics and money.

As the money-pie gets smaller in America, it will become a life or death issue who is voted into office. Study, think, vote and GIT OFF ZERO!

GITTIN' OFF ZERO

"It is unfortunate, too, that such a large number of
Negroes do not know any better than to stake
their whole fortune on politics. History does not show that
any race, especially a minority group,
has ever solved an important problem by relying
altogether on one thing, certainly not by parking
its political strength on one side of the fence because of
empty promises. There are Negroes who
know better, but such thinkers are kept in the background
by the traducers of the race to prevent
the enlightenment of the masses. The misleading
politicians are the only persons through whom
the traducers act with respect to the Negro, and there are
always a sufficient number of mentally
undeveloped voters who will supply them a large
following."

-Carter G. Woodson
The MIs-education of the Negro

CHAPTER 9

<u>STANDARDS</u>

'I ain't got a penny but I want a dime piece!'

GITTIN' OFF ZERO

"The schools in which Negroes are now being trained, however, do not give our young people this point of view. They may occasionally learn the elements of stenography and accounting, but they do not learn how to apply what they have studied. The training which they undergo gives a false   conception of life when they believe that the business world owes them a position of leadership.

They have the idea of business training that we used to have of teaching when it was thought that we could teach anything we had studied. Graduates of our business schools lack the courage to throw themselves upon their resources and work for a commission. The large majority of them want to be sure of receiving a certain amount at the end of the week or month. They do not seem to realize that the great strides in business have been made by paying men according to what they do. Persons with such false impressions of life are not good representatives of schools of business administration.

Not long ago a firm of Washington, D. C., appealed to the graduates of several of our colleges and offered them an inviting proposition on the commission basis, but only five of the hundreds appealed to respond and only two of the five gave satisfaction. Another would have succeeded, but he was not honest in handling money because he had learned to purloin the treasury of the athletic organization while in college. All of the others, however, were anxious to serve somewhere in an office for a small wage a week.

Recently one of the large insurance companies selected for special training in this line fifteen college graduates of our accredited institutions and financed their special training in insurance.

GITTIN' OFF ZERO

Only one of the number, however, rendered efficient service in this field. They all abandoned the effort after a few days' trial and accepted work in hotels and with the Pullman Company, or they went into teaching or something else with a fixed stipend until they could enter upon the practice of professions. The thought of the immediate reward, shortsightedness, and the lack of vision and courage to struggle and win the fight made them failures to begin with. They are unwilling to throw aside their coats and collars and do the groundwork of Negro business and thus make opportunities for themselves instead of begging others for a chance."

-Carter G. Woodson
The Mis-education of the Negro

The term 'dime piece' refers to a beautiful, well-shaped, woman. This term is often used by Black men in the hood to describe the kind of women they want. Yet, many of those men who say they seek these ultra-sexy women do not find it necessary to have anything to offer besides a hard penis. More confusing is many of these sexy women, in the Black community accepts, tolerates and yes, sleeps with these men who can only offer a few minutes of pleasure in bed. I will call it as I see it. Many Black Americans have let standard levels of relationships slip so low that anything goes.

It confuses me to no end that so many African Americans who are consumed with the idea of wealth and power; or being a 'baller' as the kids say. Yet when they go to choose a date or mate, they have no standards. I understand socioeconomic issues that go into these thought patterns. Brothers, before you can be of service to any young women, be of service to yourself. Get some money, save some money and put yourself in a position to look out for women that have more to offer than just 15 minutes of pleasure. Sisters, many of you have too many bills too many children and too many problems to be spreading your legs for a man that has more problems than you.

GITTIN' OFF ZERO

I know that many of the low standards and dysfunctions of the hood come from low self-esteem, low education levels, lack of role models and many of the issue we have spoken about in other chapters of Gittin off Zero. I have to put it out there; Black men cannot be the enemy of Black women. Black women cannot be the competition for Black men. Black America in particular, is at a crossroad. Gentleman, remember this: You will never lose any women chasing money but you can lose a lot of money chasing women. Women, remember this: Your body is a gift from God. Cherish it; nurses make way more money than strippers. I have nothing against strippers, but I do not think it should be career option number one for your daughter. Upgrade your standards and GIT OFF ZERO.

P.S. Did I say that I have nothing against strippers?

'In this untoward situation the Negro finds himself at the close of the third generation from Emancipation. He has been educated in the sense that persons directed a certain way are more easily controlled, or as Ovid remarked, "In time the bull is brought to bear the yoke." The Negro in this state continues as a child. He is restricted in his sphere to small things, and with these he becomes satisfied. His ambition does not rise any higher than to plunge into the competition with
his fellows for these trifles"

-Carter G. Woodson
The MIs-education of the Negro

Chapter 10
CONCLUSION

"History shows, then, that as a result of these
unusual forces in the education of the Negro he
easily learns to follow the line of least resistance rather
than battle against odds for what real
history has shown to be the right course. A mind that
remains in the present atmosphere never
undergoes sufficient development to experience what is
commonly known as thinking. No Negro
thus submerged in the ghetto, then, will have a clear
conception of the present status of the race
or sufficient foresight to plan for the future; and he drifts
so far toward compromise that he loses
moral courage. The education of the Negro, then,
becomes a perfect device for control from
without. Those who purposely promote it have every
reason to rejoice, and Negroes themselves
exultingly champion the cause of the oppressor."

-Carter G. Woodson
The MIs-education of the Negro

Big Boss Filmworks, High Exposure Consulting and GITTIN OFF ZERO ATL would like to thank you for reading this book giving us a moment of your life and letting me share my thoughts. God has been so very good to me. I could no longer hold back some insights I have about life. I want to leave you with these thoughts: You are the help you are waiting for. The only one who can stop you is you, Life is not fair but God is great and God lives in each one of us. Start acting like it! It is better to be lucky than good, but you cannot count on luck, so be good at something.

We at High Exposure Consulting are here to help. Call one of our life coaches and let us help you GIT OFF ZERO and then stay off zero. Be well and God bless!

The Million Man March, Washington, D.C., October 1995

LIFE **COACHING &** BUSINESS **CONSULTING**

The End For Now....

GITTIN' OFF ZERO

The Negroes' point of view, therefore, must be changed

before they can construct a program

which will bring them out of the wilderness. For example,

no good can be expected from one of

our teachers who said that she had to give up her class in

Sunday school to accept an extra job of

waiting on table at that hour because she had bought a

twenty-four-hundred-dollar coat and her

husband had purchased an expensive car. Such a

teacher has no message for the Negro child. Her

example would tend to drag the youth downward, and the

very thought of having such a person

in the schoolroom is most depressing.

We must feel equally discouraged when we see a

minister driving up to his church on Sunday

morning in a Cadillac. He does not come to feed the

multitude spiritually. He comes to fleece the

flock. The appeal he makes is usually emotional. While

the people are feeling happy the

expensive machine is granted, and the prolonged

vacation to use it is easily financed. Thus the

thoughtless drift backward toward slavery.

-Carter G. Woodson

The MIs-education of the Negro

QUOTES

TO THNK ABOUT

At this moment, then, the Negroes must begin to do the very thing which they have been taught that they cannot do. They still have some money, and they have needs to supply. They must begin immediately to pool their earnings and organize industries to participate in supplying social and economic demands. If the Negroes are to remain forever removed from the producing atmosphere, and the present discrimination continues, there will be nothing left for them to do.

-Carter G. Woodson
The Mis-education of the Negro

"The wrath of man shall praise thee." If the Negro in the ghetto must eternally be fed by the hand that pushes him into the ghetto, he will never become strong enough to get out of the ghetto. This assumption of Negro leadership in the ghetto, then, must not be confined to matters of religion, education, and social uplift; it must deal with such fundamental forces in life as make these things possible. If the Negro area, however, is to continue as a district supported wholly from without, the inept dwellers therein will merit and will receive only the contempt of those who may occasionally catch glimpses of them in their plight.

-Carter G. Woodson
The MIs-education of the Negro

"The undesirable aspect of the affair is that the Negro in spite of the changes from one method of approach to that of another is never brought into the inner circle of the party with which he is affiliated. He is always kept on the outside and is used as a means to an end. To obtain the meager consideration which he receives the Negro must work clandestinely through the back door. It has been unnecessary for the white man to change this procedure, for until recent years he has generally found it possible to satisfy the majority of Negroes with the few political positions earmarked as "Negro jobs" and to crush those who clamor for more recognition.

-Carter G. Woodson
The MIs-education of the Negro

'Even the few Negroes who are elected to office are often similarly uninformed and show a lack of vision. They have given little attention to the weighty problems of the nation; and in the legislative bodies to which they are elected; they restrict themselves as a rule to matters of special concern to the Negroes themselves, such as lynching, segregation and disfranchisement, which they have well learned by experience. This indicates a step backwards, for the Negroes who sat in Congress and in the State Legislatures during the reconstruction worked for the enactment of measures of concern to all elements of the population regardless of color. Historians have not yet forgot what those Negro statesmen did in advocating public education, internal improvements, labor arbitration, the tariff, and the merchant marine."

-Carter G. Woodson
The MIs-education of the Negro

"We have appealed to the talented tenth for a remedy, but they have nothing to offer. Their minds have never functioned in this all-important sphere. The "educated" Negro shows no evidence of vision. He should see a new picture. The Negroes are facing the alternative of rising in the sphere of production to supply their proportion of the manufacturers and merchants or of going down to the graves of paupers. The Negro must now do for himself or die out as the world undergoes readjustment. If the whites are to continue for some time in doing drudgery to the exclusion of Negroes, the latter must find another way out. Nothing forces this upon one more dramatically than when he learns that white women in Montgomery, Alabama, are coming to the back door of Negro homes asking for their washing. If the whites have reached this extremity, and they must be taken care of first, what will be left for the Negroes?"

-Carter G. Woodson
The MIs-education of the Negro

"The system, therefore, has extended from one thing to another until the Negroes today find themselves hedged in by the color bar almost every way they turn; and, set off by themselves, the Negroes cannot learn from the example of others with whom they might come into contact. In the ghetto, too, they are not permitted to construct and carry out a program of their own. These segregating institutions interfere with the development of self-help among Negroes, for often Negroes fail to raise money to establish institutions which they might control, but they readily contribute large sums for institutions which segregate persons of African blood."

-Carter G. Woodson
The MIs-education of the Negro

GITTIN' OFF ZERO WORK BOOK

1. What is your dream?

2. What are you doing to work towards that dream?

3. Are you in debt?

4. Do you have a plan to get out of debt?

5. Are you satisfied with your formal education status?

6. Do you think you need more formal education?

7. 1 year goal

    3 year goal

    5 year goal

8. On a scale of 1 to 10 rate your personal life?

9. On a scale of 1 to 10 how would you rate your family life?

10. Do you have a savings account?

11. Do you want to be self-employed?

12 Do you have a savings plan?

13. Do you have children?

14. What is the biggest barrier to living your dream?

15. Who is your hero?

16. Where do you see yourself in 5 years

17. If you had 10 million dollars, no debt yet only10 years to live with perfect health what would you do?

18. Have you ever written a business plan?

19. What would be an ideal day if money and time were not an issue?

20. What are your strong suits?

Everyone needs a dream and a reason to get up and leave the house. To Quote the Chinese proverbs, "find a job you love and you'll never work a day in your life."

Email or mail typed responses to the workbook and we will review and respond as soon as possible.

highexposureconsulting@yahoo.com

Big Boss Books

PO Box 250464

Franklin, MI 48025

Courtney R Brown JR.
About The Author

Courtney R. Brown Jr., C.E.O of Big Boss Filmworks, Big Boss Books and numerous other enterprises. Mr. Brown went to NYC College and graduated WMU. Mr. Brown has travelled the world and has done business worldwide. Mr. Brown grew up in a life of privileged yet never lost touch with the struggle of his people. Now an accomplished film maker, author and business consultant, Mr. Brown and Big Boss Filmworks and Books are committed to using their unique life experiences to depict the urban experience. His mission is to tell the truth of life in the struggle.

Gittin Off Zero

In the Beginning:

The Raymond Tatum Story

(GOZ)GITTIN'OFF ZERO originated in Atlanta Georgia in the early 1980s the street phrase GOZ was use by myself and associate. The phrase inspired my imagination as well as my self determination to create the company (GOZ)GITTIN' OFF ZERO Inc. As a disabled Vietnam veteran, That received the Purple Heart as a result of injuries in South Vietnam April of 1969 the phrase has been a motivating force in my life over the years. While on patrol in April of 1969 in the jungle of South Vietnam we came upon a Viet Cong base camp. The Viet Cong typically booby trapped these camps before they abandoned them, nevertheless our job was to search the camp and destroy any Viet Cong ammo dumps we found. I was carrying the m-60 machine gun which kept me in the middle of the formation as we patrolled the area. We moved into the camp and I was behind three or more troops in the formation, which I had hoped would minimize any risk of injury in this particular situation. The trail was hard to follow as we investigated the camp. As we we're leaving, trying as best we could to back track on the same trail we entered, there was a loud deafening shatter of an explosion and after a couple of seconds I realized I was hit. It was a landmine.

After immediately falling to the ground unaware of what exactly had happened, I could feel an unexplainable and painful burning sensation coming from my left ankle. I needed to see what was causing me so much pain. I looked and the front half of my left foot was gone. I was bleeding profusely from the dismembered main artery that lead down my left leg. Fortunately the medic was able to get to me and apply a tourniquet above my knee to stop the heavy bleeding. Doc, the medic, gave me a shot of morphine to reduce the pain. Two of my buddies carried me out of the bush and put me on the chopper that had come to take me to the rear where the main field hospital was located. While on the chopper another medic asked if I was in any pain, I said yes and he gave me another shot of morphine. Later I would find that I had received more injuries other than the loss of a foot, but at the time the pain at the lower part of my ankle dominated all other feelings and emotions going through my mind and body.

That day along with other experiences in south Vietnam changed the course of my life forever, both mentally and physically. I would never be the same.

(GOZ)GITTIN' OFF ZERO has been a process that has evolved over the years it begin as an attraction to the expression / phrase itself. GOZ Came out of an environment of the streets And all the activity That goes with that Lifestyle, the guy I heard say it That had the greatest Impact On me, was a old hustler by the name of (Jessie Cup Davis) it was just the way he said it that inspired or impressed me. The phrase GOZ was first Expressed As GITTIN' ME OFF ZERO But that expression / Phrase seem to imply to look for something outside of myself, however The expression / Phrase GITTIN' OFF ZERO Implies Self-determination or look within. After being discharged from the military at Fort Gordon Hospital in Augusta Georgia in December of 1969 my oldest brother Sweet was stationed at Fort Bragg North Carolina, He and my brother Lee had made it possible earlier for us to move around the Fayetteville North Carolina Hustlin community without a whole lot of problems. Sweet came and got me and said he needed some help in running a house he was hustling out of, so I went and my other brother, Reginald came later we were living outside of Fayetteville in a place call Spring lake, we were hustling out of a house where all kinds of things was going on, drugs, alcohol, gambling, prostitution you name it, we got out of that town by the grace of the good lawd, because my MOTHER didn't raise us that way.After getting out of Fayetteville North Carolina alive we came back to Atlanta Georgia and I started school on the GI bill but I was still struggling to cope with the psychological results of my injuries in Vietnam by using drugs and alcohol and couldn't apply myself so I gave up and gave in to drugs and alcohol,

When I first design the logo I did not know anything about starting a business I just got started, getting information from anywhere I could I thought it was a good idea and just started to make it happen I found a silk screen artist and had a few t-shirt printed. To see my idea come to life was awesome it made me feel great, I began to show the t-shirts to friends and trying to sell them. It felt good to have somebody like my idea and actually pay me for the product. I stayed focused for a while and found myself back in the grip of addiction ripping and running behind drugs and alcohol again, and doing a lot of illegal things to maintain my drug and alcohol problem, this led to going in and out of jail an ultimately to a stitch in prison, after serving 33 months on a 10 ten year sentence I was paroled, my experience in prison taught me that prison wasn't for me. After being released a partner of mine name the thin man I had used drugs with; had turned preacher before I went to prison and I have a great deal of respect for him. The thin man had bought a truck and started a rolling store, he came and talk with me after I was released and let me know what he was doing and out of that meeting we decided to do something together, he already had the rolling store so he decided to bring me in, we needed a name for the rolling store so the thin man ask me to come up with a design for the name he call ("grits on wheels") after I finished the logo I put it with some artwork I had done before I went to prison And the gittin' me off zero logo was part of that artwork so I put ("grits on wheels") logo with the artwork and slid it back under my bed. When the thin man came to see the ("grits on wheels") logo, when I pulled the artwork from underneath the bed, he looked at it and as he was looking at it the gittin me off zero logo caught his eye and he ask me what was that and I told him that was my gittin' me off zero logo I designed before I went to prison he looked at me with a great deal of excitement and said that's the name of the rolling store, Gittin' me off zero.

The Thin man and I, with the help of one of our associate name (Buster) who was in the game give us a small loan and we had some product printed up and posted up on Georgia Avenue in the community we was raised in called Summerhill. The part of Georgia Avenue we posted up on was where all the twisting and turning was going on, in the process the thin man upgraded the truck to a larger one and we had the gittin' me off zero logo put on both sides and went to rollin. Again I stayed focus for a while and with a little success with GOZ I lost sight and started back using drugs and alcohol again. As a result of my using a strain was put on the thin man and my relationship, I continued to market GOZ myself with the help of another one of my associates named (Frank) who also liked the gittin' me off zero idea, Frank was good people but unfortunately Frank had a substance abuse problem as well, Again I found myself back in trouble with the law, I manage to get some probation stacked on top of probation and my probation officer gave me an alternative. I could either go into a drug treatment program or go back to jail. so I chose to go in to a drug program and he sent me to the VA hospital so I decided enough is enough I would get my life together and resurrect GITTIN' OFF ZERO this was in 1991 and over the years I have redesigned the logo fine tuned it's meaning, added and deleted product, marketed the product on consignment, create a website, I currently operate a kiosks downtown in Atlanta Georgia at Peachtree Street and Decatur Street at Five points, I also promote GOZ on Facebook and Instagram, contact me @ WWW.GITTINOFFZERO.COM

Although (GOZ)GITTIN' OFF ZERO seems to have originated from a negative environment, for me it has evolved into something richer, although the expression in it's

origin was like finding a diamond in the rough, as a disable Vietnam vet who lost a foot in South Vietnam and lives with PTSD and recovering from substance abuse for the last 21 years the expression has been and is a powerful tool in my recovery process. The expression / phrase has revealed to me that we all have diamonds in the rough inside of us, these diamonds can be expressed in a variety of ways, Mentally,

Spiritually, Physically, Intellectually, Financially, Politically or Socially. GITTIN' OFF ZERO is the starting point of ones goals, aspirations and Dreams, GO GIT IT!

BE ON THE LOOKOUT FOR FUTURE PROJECTS

FROM

BIG BOSS BOOKS AND BIG BOSS FILMWORKS.

Big Man On Campus

Corey Black Jr. is a newly pledged frat member, who is in college to make his Mother happy and proud to be the first man in the family to go to college. He is also the son and nephew of two of Detroit's most notorious drug kingpins. His Father Corey Black who has fled authorities and his uncle Joe Black who is the reigning figure in the narcotics trade. Uncle Joe has Corey do "runs" for him, to carry on the family 'business' running narcotics and laundering money. Uncle Joe also owns real estate with Corey's Mother Tracy who has great deal of control in the business.

Corey Black Sr. wanted Corey to go to school to bring legitimacy to the family. While in College Corey Jr. with the help of his friends and girlfriend start and grow a successful drug operation, unbeknownst to Uncle Joe and Tracy. Corey enjoys the most exclusive strip clubs, frat parties, casinos and women that the city has to offer, while basking in his new found popularity. Corey finds himself conflicted with his responsibility to running the family "business" and his obligation to his college studies. However, he'll have to make things work in his favor if he wants to remain... *BIG MAN ON CAMPUS*

BOOK AND FILM COMING SOON

FILM COMING SOON

Gittin' Off Zero

There are more African American men in jail than in college. The unemployment rate among African American men in most major cities is 70%. The African American infant mortality rates are at third world levels. How did we get here? Could these statistics apply to the descendants of the great West African king and controller of the world's gold and salt distribution of his day, Mansa Musa or to the descendants of Detroit's Black Bottom, The Harlem Renaissance or Black Wall Street in Tulsa Oklahoma?

Hi I am Courtney R. Brown Jr., C.E.O of Big Boss Filmworks, Big Boss Books, Isaiah Properties, African Nights INC., High Exposure Consulting and a consultant for Bridge fort, INC., a family business. You may ask. Why so many companies? Well in today's world a man or woman may need to have 3 or 4 hustles or AKA enterprises to be able to live the lifestyle they want. The Advantage of this is when one enterprise aka hustle slows, another will be busy. Seldom will all the enterprises aka hustles be slow at the same time

We at Big Boss Filmworks and Big Boss Books have decided to do this project, "Gittin' Off Zero" because of the current state of many African American people in our major cities, Detroit Michigan, in particular; Why Detroit? Well two reasons. First I am from Detroit and the current situations of senseless murders and nation leading unemployment rate makes the lessons and life skills mentioned in this project a desperately needed answer for a troubled people in a troubling time. Why am I qualified to speak on the issues of transforming the street hustler mentality into a legitimate business model?

GITTIN' OFF ZERO

First let me give you some background on myself. A member of my family was an integral part of the largest drug ring in Detroit's history. I grew up in the plush suburbs after moving from the projects. My family was able to live a life of luxury from the profits of this family member's underworld activity. So when I say I understand the streets take my word for it. That family member was sent to a federal prison where we visited him frequently. So when I say I know the downside of the streets take my word for it. I have managed a 12 million dollar a year store in New York. I have worked on the nation's most exclusive shopping streets, Madison Ave. and Columbus Ave. in New York; I have owned and operated stores in Harlem N.Y., Atlanta GA and Detroit Mi. I introduced the Coogi and Joe Boxer lines of clothing to Harlem N.Y. I have done business in China, Europe and the Caribbean. I have traveled the world vacationing. So when I say i understand how startup businesses and international trade has changed the world for all of us, take my word for it.

Enough about me let's talk about you, your brother, sister, father or uncle. Are you or your family suffering from the effects of this country's latest recession? If you are, you know that for African American males this current economic condition is not a recession but a depression, with unemployment among Black men ranging from 30-70% depending on whose stats you use. I am going to use Detroit as an example, but these conditions can be applied to Philadelphia, L.A., Atlanta or any other big city. Thus to understand where we are we must know where we came from. A person with no history is a person with no future. So for a moment let's go back in history: Way back like 685 years ago. In the year 1323

GITTIN' OFF ZERO

685 years ago an African king named Mansa Musa controlled a West African gold empire that sold gold to Europe and Asia and Set the price of gold throughout most of the world. Yes we as a people have always loved gold.

Gittin' Off Zero will lay out a blueprint of how to turn the hustler mentality into a corporate business model that will lead to prosperous African American families, neighborhoods and businesses.

The Crowd Pleaser: Eddie 'The Fat Man' Jackson

The Original Rain Man

The Crowd Pleaser is the exploits of Eddie "The Fat Man" Jackson told through his son Eddie Jackson Jr. in the revealing book of Mr. Jackson's rise from a broke taxi driver, to becoming Detroit's biggest drug kingpin. The story chronicles: Mr. Jackson's partnership with Courtney "The Field Marshall" Brown, the mafia, his global jet setting lifestyle, his interaction with music and movie elite from The Temptations, Sammy Davis Jr., Redd Foxx, Richard Pryor to Donald Goines and his 7 year legal battle that is taken to the Supreme Court.

Find out how he helped build "The Urban Empire" and live the life that rappers emulate today. Find out why Eddie Jackson was a much larger figure than Frank Lucas. Find out how he earned the nicknames "The Crowd Pleaser" and "Rain Man". The book also documents never before told secrets and life lessons from Mr. Jackson to Eddie Jackson Jr.

GITTIN' OFF ZERO

THE
KINGPIN'S KID
WITTEN BY LEWIS STEVENS AND COURTNEY R. BROWN JR.

Based On A True Story.

BIG BOSS

FILM COMING SOON

The Kingpin's Kid

By Lewis F. Stevens & Courtney R. Brown Jr.

The Kingpin's Kid is the memoir of Courtney Brown Jr., chronicling the rise and fall of his father, Courtney "Berman" Brown Sr., and his Partner Eddie "Fat Man" Jackson. The pair start from meager beginnings to rustling control of the Detroit drug trade and attaining millions and millions of dollars, while raising their families in the background of girl and boy scouts, little league baseball, while attempting to avoid Federal law enforcement. Based on the book "Motown Mafia."

GITTIN' OFF ZERO APPAREL

ATLANTA, GA.
Gittinoffzero.com

Submission Guidelines

To all interested Authors wanting to submit manuscripts for possible consideration. Please follow the below listed guidelines.

1. We request a brief but detailed synopsis.

2. The first four chapters are also required.

3. Double spaced, one side of page if possible,

   12pt. or greater.

4. Margins and semi-formatting.

5. No photo copies unless extremely clear and legible.

6. Please enclose all contact information; e-mail, phone, mailing address, etc.

7. Absolutely no electronic submissions accepted.

MAIL TO

P.O. BOX 250464

FRANKLIN, MICHIGAN 48025

248-619-6509

No Submissions Will Be Returned.

Please don't contact us for status updates.

We will be in touch in 45-60 days.

BIG BOSS BOOKS

P.O. BOX 250464

FRANKLIN, MICHIGAN 48025

248-619-6509

<u>ORDER FORM</u>

NAME:

ADDRESS:

CITY:

STATE: ZIP CODE:

QTY. PRICE	TITLE	
	Motown Mafia	$16.99
	Gittin' Off Zero	$16.99
N/A	The Kingpin's Kid	
N/A	The Crowd Pleaser	
N/A	Big Man On Campus	

TOTAL_____

Make all Money Orders, Personal Checks and Institutional Checks payable to- **Big Boss Books**. Please allow 7-10 days for delivery after receipt of order.

P.O. BOX 250464

FRANKLIN, MICHIGAN 48025

GITTIN' OFF ZERO

ORDER FORM

NAME:

ADDRESSS:

CITY:

STATE: ZIP CODE:

QTY.	TITLE	PRICE
	Motown Mafia	$16.99
	Gittin' Off Zero	$16.99
N/A	The Kingpin's Kid	
N/A	The Crowd Pleaser	
N/A	Big Man On Campus	

TOTAL_____

Make all Money Orders, Personal Checks and Institutional Checks payable to- **Big Boss Books.** Please allow 7-10 days for delivery after receipt of order.

Works Cited

Page 18 Robison, Randall An Unbroken Agony page 62 Basic Civitas Books, 2007

Page 24 Woodson, Carter G. Mis-Education of the Negro. Buffalo N.Y.: EWorld INC, 1933.

Page Kimbro,Denis, Daily meditations Random House Publishing Group Publication date: 10/12/2011

Page 52 Woodson, Carter G. Mis-Education of the Negro. Page 109 Buffalo N.Y.: EWorld INC, 1933.

Page 58-63 Woodson, Carter G. Mis-Education of the Negro. Page 80-81 Buffalo N.Y.: EWorld INC, 1933.

Page 66 Woodson, Carter G. Mis-Education of the Negro. Page 5 Buffalo N.Y.: EWorld INC, 1933.

Page 72 Woodson, Carter G. Mis-Education of the Negro. Page 15 Buffalo N.Y.: EWorld INC, 1933.

Page 78 Woodson, Carter G. Mis-Education of the Negro. Page 87 Buffalo N.Y.: EWorld INC, 1933.

GITTIN' OFF ZERO

Page 81 Woodson, Carter G. <u>Mis-Education of the Negro</u>. Page 94 Buffalo N.Y.: EWorld INC, 1933.

Page 83- 84 Woodson, Carter G. <u>Mis-Education of the Negro</u>. Page 46-48 Buffalo N.Y.: EWorld INC, 1933.

Page 87 Woodson, Carter G. <u>Mis-Education of the Negro</u>. Page 111 Buffalo N.Y.: EWorld INC, 1933.

Page 89 Woodson, Carter G. <u>Mis-Education of the Negro</u>. Page 96 Buffalo N.Y.: EWorld INC, 1933.

Page 91-92 Woodson, Carter G. <u>Mis-Education of the Negro</u>. Page 124 Buffalo N.Y.: EWorld INC, 1933.

Page 93 Woodson, Carter G. <u>Mis-Education of the Negro</u>. Page 108 Buffalo N.Y.: EWorld INC, 1933.

Page 94 Woodson, Carter G. <u>Mis-Education of the Negro</u>. Page 110 Buffalo N.Y.: EWorld INC, 1933.

Page 95 Woodson, Carter G. <u>Mis-Education of the Negro</u>. Page 93 Buffalo N.Y.: EWorld INC, 1933.

Page 96 Woodson, Carter G. <u>Mis-Education of the Negro</u>. 94-95 Buffalo N.Y.: EWorld INC, 1933.

Page 97 Woodson, Carter G. <u>Mis-Education of the Negro</u>. Page 107 Buffalo N.Y.: EWorld INC, 1933.

Page 98 Woodson, Carter G. <u>Mis-Education of the Negro</u>.
104 Buffalo N.Y.: EWorld INC, 1933.

WEALTH, HAPPINESS & PROSPERITY HIDING IN PLAIN SIGHT....

"A mind that remains in the present atmosphere never undergoes sufficient development to experience what is commonly known as thinking."

"When you control a man's thinking you do not have to worry about his actions. You do not have to tell him not to stand here or go yonder. He will find his "proper place" and will stay in it. You do not need to send him to the back of the back door. He will go without being told. In fact, if there is no back door, he will cut one for his special benefit. His education makes it necessary."

COURTNEY R BROWN JR.
AUTHOR & ENTREPRENEUR

RAYMOND TATUM
FOUNDER OF GOZ ATL

-CARTER G. WOODSON THE MISEDUCATION OF THE NEGRO

bigbossfilmworks.com $16.99

ISBN 978-0-9828506-1-9

P.o. Box 250464 Franklin, Mi 48025 TEL: 248.619.6509 313.408.5366
EMAIL: bigbossfilmworks@yahoo.com

GITTIN' OFF ZERO

Made in the USA
Columbia, SC
11 November 2024

45989816R00070